DATE DUE

	Angelica		

From Egg to Adult
The Life Cycle of Amphibians

Richard and Louise
Spilsbury

Heinemann Library
Chicago, Illinois

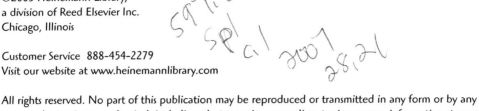

Customer Service 888-454-2279
Visit our website at www.heinemannlibrary.com

Editing, Design, Photo Research, and Production by Heinemann Library
Illustrations by David Woodroffe
Originated by Dot Gradations Ltd
Printed in China by Wing King Tong

07 06 05 04 03
10 9 8 7 6 5 4 3 2 1

Library of Congress Cataloging-in-Publication Data
Spilsbury, Louise.
  The life cycle of amphibians / Louise & Richard Spilsbury.
     p. cm. -- (From egg to adult)
Summary: Discusses how amphibians differ from other animals, their habitat, how they are born and develop, what they eat, how they reproduce, and their typical life expectancy.
Includes bibliographical references (p.   ).
  ISBN 1-4034-0785-1 (HC) 1-4034-3403-4 (PB)
  1. Amphibians--Life cycles--Juvenile literature. [1. Amphibians.] I. Spilsbury, Richard, 1963-   . II. Title. III. Series.
  QL644.2 .S72 2003
  597.8--dc21
                          2002011705

Acknowledgments
The Publishers would like to thank the following for permission to reproduce photographs:
pp. 5, 6, 15 Bruce Coleman Collection/Jane Burton; p. 7 Oxford Scientific Films/Paulo De Oliveira; p. 8 Bruce Coleman/Kim Taylor; pp. 9 (bottom), 21 Oxford Scientific Films; p. 10 NHPA/James Carmichael Jr.; pp. 11, 14, 25 NHPA/Stephen Dalton; p. 12 (top) FLPA/Treat Davidson; p. 12 (bottom) Oxford Scientific Films/Marty Cordano; p. 13 NHPA/Karl Switak; p. 16 Ardea/Peter Steyn; p. 17 Oxford Scientific Films/Juan M Renjifo; p. 18 Oxford Scientific Films/Mantis Wildlife Films; pp. 19, 24 NHPA/Daniel Heuclin; p. 20 NHPA/Roger Tidman; p. 22 NHPA/Ant Photo Library; p. 23 Oxford Scientific Films/P J Devries; p. 26 FLPA/Minden Pictures.

Cover photograph of the common frogs reproduced with permission of Bruce Coleman Collection.

The frog at the top of each page is a red-eyed tree frog.

Every effort has been made to contact copyright holders of any material reproduced in this book. Any omissions will be rectified in subsequent printings if notice is given to the Publishers.

Some words are shown in bold, **like this.** You can find out what they mean by looking in the glossary.

Contents

What Is an Amphibian? .4

How Are Amphibians Born? 5

Who Takes Care of Baby Amphibians? 9

How Do Baby Amphibians Grow Bigger? 11

How Do Amphibians Grow Up Safely? 15

When Are Amphibians Grown Up? 19

How Do Amphibians Have Babies? 20

How Old Do Amphibians Get? 25

Fact File 28

Amphibian Classification 29

Glossary 30

More Books to Read .31

Index 32

Look but don't touch: Many amphibians are easily hurt but also have poisonous skin. If you see one in the wild, do not get too close to it. Look at it, but do not try to touch it!

What Is an Amphibian?

Amphibians are animals such as frogs that usually live one part of their lives in water and another part on land. Amphibians have soft skin without scales or hair. The skin is usually covered in a slippery fluid called **mucus.** Most amphibians breathe both through their moist skin and through lungs or **gills.**

Amphibians are **vertebrates.** A vertebrate is an animal with a backbone that supports its body. Amphibians are cold-blooded, which means that their bodies are only as warm or cold as their surroundings.

frog

salamander

caecilian

Three groups of amphibians

There are more than 4,000 different **species** of amphibians on Earth. They are divided into three groups—frogs and toads, salamanders and newts, and caecilians.

This picture shows adult examples of the three groups of amphibians. Frogs and toads have no tails, large heads and eyes, and long back legs. Newts and salamanders resemble lizards, with tails, small eyes, and usually equal length legs. Caecilians, or blind worms, have no eyes, no legs, and usually no tail. They look much more like giant earthworms or snakes than other amphibians!

How Are Amphibians Born?

When baby amphibians are born, they usually hatch from eggs. These eggs are round and less than a half inch (one centimeter) across. The middle of the egg is the **yolk.** Part of the yolk develops into an **embryo,** which becomes the baby amphibian. The embryo becomes bigger and stronger by using the rest of the yolk as food.

Protective covering

The outer covering of an amphibian egg is usually soft, clear, and jellylike. This covering cushions the developing embryo. It also keeps it from drying out. If embryos dry out, they usually die.

*These are frog eggs. The black spots are the parts that develop into young frog forms called **larvae.***

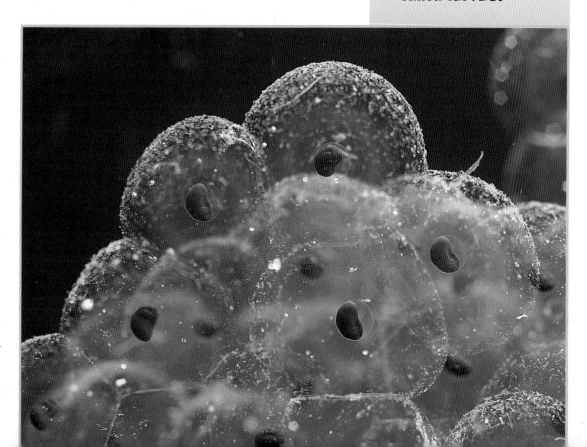

Amphibians lay their eggs in wet places, such as the calm waters of a pond. This keeps them from drying out. The eggs are sticky. They stay safe by sticking to each other, plants, or rocks.

Some amphibians, such as toads, lay their eggs in sticky strings about three feet (one meter) long. Others, such as frogs, produce hundreds or even thousands of eggs that cling together in floating masses of jelly called frogspawn. Others lay much smaller numbers of eggs.

Some amphibians, such as the common toad, wrap their strings of eggs around water plants so the eggs do not drift away.

Breaking free

It takes about two weeks for most amphibian **embryos** to fully develop. Some amphibians may take longer to develop than others. The weather can affect the time development takes. If it is too cold, eggs may take much longer to hatch. In hot, dry places where ponds only appear for a short time after a rainy season, it may take months before it is wet enough for eggs to hatch.

When they are ready to hatch, the **larvae** wriggle and twist. This movement breaks open the jelly covering around the eggs and the larvae swim out.

Salamander larvae wriggle to break out of their eggs.

Odd ones out

Some frogs, salamanders, and caecilians give birth to live young. The eggs stay inside the female's body and the embryos develop there, protected from the world outside. The young are actually born after they have hatched from their eggs inside the mother.

What do new baby amphibians look like?

Many amphibian **larvae** look like tiny fish when they hatch.
Frog and toad larvae are usually called tadpoles. A tadpole
that has just hatched is about half as long as your little
fingernail. Its head and body form a wide lump with a narrow
tail attached. It has no legs or arms. Two or three pairs of
feathery **gills** grow behind its head.

Breathing underwater with gills

Most amphibian larvae and all fish have gills to breathe
underwater. Gills contain **blood vessels** surrounded by thin
skin. Water contains **oxygen,** an element that nearly all
animals need to live. When water flows over gills, oxygen goes
into the blood vessels. Blood carries the oxygen throughout
an animal's body. It also helps to take wastes away from the
animal's body.

*A newt larva is
shaped kind of like
an adult, but it has
three pairs of gills
and weak, skinny
legs. As the larva
grows up, it changes.*

Who Takes Care of Baby Amphibians?

Most amphibians never know their parents. After the eggs are laid and **fertilized,** the parents go elsewhere, often out of the water. The larvae are left on their own.

Dangers

Life is dangerous for amphibian larvae. Most of them do not live through their first few days or weeks. They are small and weak, so they cannot move quickly, nor can they see much. This makes it easy for **predators,** such as fish, to catch and eat them.

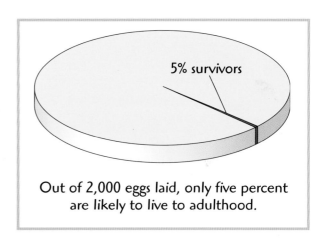

5% survivors

Out of 2,000 eggs laid, only five percent are likely to live to adulthood.

Staying alive

Larvae usually stay still at first to try to avoid being seen. Frog larvae attach themselves to water plants, often in the shade. They feed at first on the **yolk** in their stomachs, which is left over from their time inside the egg.

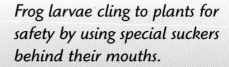

Frog larvae cling to plants for safety by using special suckers behind their mouths.

sucker

A safer start

A few amphibians take care of their young **larvae** to give them a safer start in life. This takes time and energy, but it means the youngsters are more likely to grow up to become adults.

Some frogs carry their larvae until they can survive on their own. Frogs that carry their young inside their mouths or stomachs are called mouth brooders or stomach brooders. After the tadpoles of the Darwin's frog hatch, the father swallows them! He is not eating them. He's just providing a safe, moist place where the young can spend their first few days.

The tadpole of this arrow-poison frog uses its sucker to cling to its parent's back.

Model parent

The female spot-bellied dart frog lays three or four eggs on the moist ground in the **tropical rain forest.** When they hatch, she carries the tadpoles on her back to tiny pools of water in the center of **bromeliad** plants. She then lays eggs in the water for the tadpoles to eat.

How Do Baby Amphibians Grow Bigger?

Amphibian larvae need to find food to grow bigger. As they grow, the larvae also gradually change shape. This change of shape is called **metamorphosis.**

Body changes

Adult frogs and toads look totally different from tadpoles. Tadpoles have no legs and a long tail that is **adapted,** or specially designed, for swimming in water. Adult frogs and toads have no tail, and legs to walk, hop, or crawl on land.

Among many salamanders and caecilians, larvae and adults look very similar to each other, except for their size. This is because when they hatch they are already adapted to the place where they will spend all their lives.

*Some salamanders, such as this axolotl and some mud puppies, live in water all their lives—from egg to adult. They have **gills** throughout their lives and some grow only tiny legs.*

During **metamorphosis,** a bullfrog tadpole's tail gradually disappears and its back legs form. A flap of skin grows over its gills, and lungs develop inside. The bullfrog can then breathe when it is out of water.

By the time it is ready to leave the water, the young bullfrog's front legs have grown. Its head, eyes, and mouth are bigger, and its back legs have grown longer and stronger. Its **webbed** feet make it a strong swimmer.

A change of diet

Salamander and newt **larvae** are **carnivores,** or meat eaters, from the moment they hatch. But most amphibian larvae start off as **herbivores,** or plant eaters. During metamorphosis they become carnivores. At first, frog and toad tadpoles "graze" by using their rough lips to grind off pieces of water plants. They become strong enough to swim faster, and then they can catch floating and swimming food such as water fleas. Their jaws change shape so they can catch food, and their stomachs change so that they can **digest** meat.

What do amphibians eat?

Adult amphibians generally catch insects, spiders, small fish, worms, and slugs. Larger amphibian species, such as bullfrogs, may eat snakes, small **mammals,** and birds. Some amphibians only eat a certain food. One group of South American frogs feeds mainly on other types of frogs, but another eats mostly fruit.

This Argentine horned frog is eating a young Argentine rainbow boa.

Catching food

Most amphibians, such as giant salamanders, sit and wait for **prey** to come closer, but some toads and salamanders stalk their prey. Many caecilians **burrow** through soil and find food as they go. Frogs and toads usually flick out their sticky tongues to catch prey, but some use their hands. Amphibians have no chewing teeth so they always swallow food whole.

Amphibians such as this Bell's horned frog push down their eyeballs while eating. That motion helps squeeze larger meals down the frog's throat.

Using their senses

Amphibians use different senses to help them find food, depending on where they live. Frogs and toads have good hearing, and most adult amphibians have good eyesight to see a meal. Eyes are useless to burrowing caecilians and cave salamanders that live in the dark. They rely on touch to find food. Many amphibians can inhale, or breathe in, smells in the air, which they taste using special pits in their mouths called the Jacobson's organ.

How Do Amphibians Grow Up Safely?

Amphibians face many dangers as they grow up. One of the biggest dangers is **predators.** Many birds, fish, and reptiles rely on amphibians as food.

A quick getaway

If they sense danger, many amphibians can get away quickly. Most adult frogs have long, strong legs so they can jump away—up to ten feet (three meters) at a time! Flying frogs use their **webbed** toes like parachutes to glide from tree to tree.

Fighting back

Some amphibians try to frighten off predators. Large amphibians, such as bullfrogs and hellbender salamanders, often attack predators. The skunk frog of Venezuela makes horrible-smelling **mucus** to fend off attackers. Some newts and salamanders twist their bodies and lie still, pretending to be dead.

Common toads stand on tiptoe and suck in air to make themselves look bigger and more fierce.

Clever colors

Most amphibians use skin color to avoid **predators.** Some are **camouflaged.** This means that their coloring is similar to the places where they live. Bright-green tree frogs live among green leaves in trees. The Solomon Island leaf frog is similar in color and shape to the brown, dead leaves it lives among.

Other amphibians are brightly colored to warn predators not to eat them. For example, young eastern newts are bright red, and fire salamanders are black and yellow. Such bold colors tell predators that these amphibians are poisonous or bad tasting. Predators may try to eat such a meal once. But they usually spit it out because it tastes so bad. They remember the unpleasant experience, and in the future they are likely to avoid such food.

Arum frogs are white to hide in the new white flowers of arum lilies, but they turn brown as the flower fades and changes color.

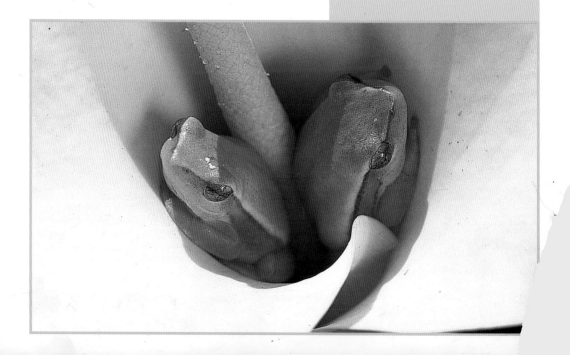

Keeping moist

Another big danger to amphibians is their skin drying out, especially if they live in hot places on land. Amphibians do not drink through their mouths—water enters their bodies mainly through their skin. To keep moist, most amphibians are active at night when it is cooler and hide in damp, cool places by day.

Keeping cool

Some amphibians find shelter from the heat in **burrows** dug by other animals, in drainpipes, or under logs. Others dig their own shelters. Spadefoot toads use their shovel-shaped feet to dig down feetfirst, but shovel-nosed frogs dig headfirst.

The tough skulls and pointed heads of caecilians are perfectly suited for digging through the soil.

Ways of breathing

Amphibians breathe partly through lungs or **gills,** but also through their skin. If their thin skin is moist, **oxygen** from the air can pass through it and move into the blood. The blood carries the oxygen to the parts of the body that need it.

Taking a break

Some amphibians take a break from hot or cold seasons by going underground. When the air is cold, soil stays warmer, and when air is hot, soil stays cooler. The Australian water-holding frog lives in deserts, where it may rain only once every seven years. It lives in a **burrow** for most of its life, only coming out when rainwater soaks the soil around it.

Surviving winter

Amphibians are cold-blooded. When it is too cool, they do not have enough energy to move around. Some, such as wood frogs, survive cold winters by **hibernating.** As they lie still in burrows under the frozen soil, their bodies shut down. They breathe slowly and do not eat until spring. A special type of sugar in their blood keeps their bodies from freezing.

The Australian water-holding frog survives underground, safe in a protective **cocoon** *made of its own* **shed** *skin. While in its cocoon, it uses water stored in its body.*

When Are Amphibians Grown Up?

An amphibian is grown up when it can start **breeding.**
That is when its body is ready to make young of its own.
Some amphibians can do this in just a few weeks or months
after **metamorphosis,** but most take longer. Common frogs
take three years, but newts take about two years.

Growing up quickly

Different amphibian **species** develop at different rates, but
the speed also depends on where they live. For example, in
places where pools of water collect only for a short time,
young amphibians have to grow up quickly.

Slowing down

Amphibians grow much more quickly during
metamorphosis than after they are grown up.
Adults do not need to eat as much or as often
as when they are young and developing rapidly.

*Chinese giant
salamanders take
about ten years to
grow up. After that,
they continue to grow
slowly as they get older.*

How Do Amphibians Have Babies?

When a male amphibian is grown up, it looks for a female to mate with. Most amphibians' eggs and **larvae** need to live in water, so most grown-up amphibians mate in wet places. They mate at times of year when it is particularly wet but also warm enough for their young to develop quickly.

Breeding places

Amphibians that live mostly on land find water by sensing how damp the air is, by smell, and also by having a good sense of direction. Some amphibian adults return to the same wet places every year, sometimes after long **migrations.** Sometimes these are the same places they were born. Great crested newts migrate up to six miles (ten kilometers) to **breeding** ponds.

The migration routes of common toads sometimes go across roads, so in some places people put up special signs warning drivers to slow down.

Finding a mate

Frogs and toads listen for calls that are similar to their own. By following these calls, they can find the right mate.

Some male amphibians set up a sheltered area called a breeding **territory** to attract a female to lay her eggs. Males then defend this area by fighting or chasing other males away.

Showing off

Many male salamanders and newts put on special "shows" called **courtship** displays to attract a mate. Some develop bright breeding colors to make them easier to see.

Perfumed partners

Axolotls are blind and deaf and live in dark underground pools. To attract males, females produce a special smell that spreads through the water.

Male great crested newts have special bright, silvery breeding colors on their tails and tall crests on their backs. The male lashes his tail back and forth to make sure a female sees him.

Calling for a partner

Frogs and toads have special **courtship** calls. Different **species** and individuals have different calls. Usually the male calls to attract a female. He fills up **vocal sacs** in his throat with air in order to make a loud sound. In a few amphibian species, it is the female that calls the male.

But calling could also attract **predators.** So most frogs and toads call at night, under the cover of darkness.

Clever males

Male frogs that make bigger sounds will attract more females. Sometimes smaller males hide near males with loud calls. They then catch any females attracted to the calls and mate with them.

The male coqui (say ko-kee) tree frog of Puerto Rico gets its name from its loud two-part call. The "kee" sound attracts females, but the "ko" sound says, "keep away" to other males.

A big hug

Once they have attracted a female, most male amphibians make sure they do not lose her before she is ready to mate. They do this by hugging her tightly. Spanish sharp-ribbed salamander males hug their females for up to 24 hours.

Many male frogs and toads have patches of rough skin on their thumbs to get a better grip on slippery females.

At mating time, a female already has eggs inside her body ready to be laid. She lays the eggs in the water, and the male **fertilizes** them by dropping his **sperm** on top.

Hitching a ride

Some male amphibians are much smaller than females of the same species. A red-eyed tree frog male calls from a tree to attract a female. When she comes to him, he grips onto her and hitches a ride to a nearby pond, where they will mate.

The male red-eyed tree frog stays close to the female until she is ready to lay her eggs.

Protecting eggs

Some amphibians hide their eggs to protect them from **predators.** Gray tree frogs make sticky foam nests in which to hide their eggs. Female newts lay about 80 sticky eggs and wrap each one up in a water plant leaf.

After a female marsupial frog lays her eggs, the male scoops them up into a pouch on her back, where they stay until the tadpoles hatch.

Many caecilians and salamanders coil their bodies around their eggs to guard them until they hatch.

Keeping eggs moist

Amphibians that lay eggs on land have to keep them from drying up. Female barking frogs lay their eggs in cracks in cliffs. The males **urinate** on the eggs to keep them moist.

The female surinam toad lays about 50 eggs in water. The eggs stick to her back and her skin grows over them for protection.

How Old Do Amphibians Get?

Most amphibians never reach old age. At all stages in an individual's life—from egg to **larva** to adult—it faces danger. As it gets older, it may be injured in fights or close calls with predators. Such injuries often make it unable to move quickly enough to avoid predators and other dangers.

A long life

Some amphibians do live for a long time, mostly in **captivity**—such as in a zoo—where there are no predators. Some Japanese giant salamanders have lived up to 55 years in captivity, growing up to 6 feet (1.8 meters) long. Others may live even longer in wild places, such as mountain rivers, which are also safe from danger.

Keeping up appearances

Amphibians, like all living things, **inherit** some features from their parents. For example, a frog usually looks like its parents. However, how it looks also depends on its **environment.** If it grows up somewhere that is dry or lacks food, it may be smaller and less healthy than its parents.

Amphibians need to be aware of danger at all times.

People and amphibians

There are some dangers that amphibians cannot avoid, whether they are young or old. People are destroying many wet places where amphibians live. Marshes and swamps are being drained so that the land can be used for farming. Water from rivers and streams is taken to **irrigate** land and to use in factories. Many **tropical rain forests** have been cut down for wood or cleared to make land for farming.

Pollution in water and in the air from factories, farms, and cars can kill many amphibians. Their moist skin easily soaks up poisons.

Disappearing acts

As different **habitats** are affected, many amphibians are becoming rare and may even become **extinct.** New types of amphibians are found each year, but it is likely that many more are disappearing without ever being discovered.

Water pollution is causing many frogs around the world to develop strangely shaped legs and eyes.

Life cycles

As amphibians slow down toward the end of their lives, they **breed** much less often and are less able to catch food. Finally, they die. The number of young an individual amphibian produces is more important to the **survival** of its **species** than how many years it lives.

Over a lifetime—if she has found suitable breeding places and males to mate with—a common toad female may have laid tens of thousands of eggs. Not all of these eggs will hatch, and not all the **larvae** will become adults. Those that then survive the challenges that life brings—such as **predators** and drying out—may eventually breed, too. This is the cycle of life—from egg to adult—in which young are born, grow, and then produce young themselves. This cycle of life ensures the survival of each amphibian species.

This picture shows the life cycle of a poison-dart frog.

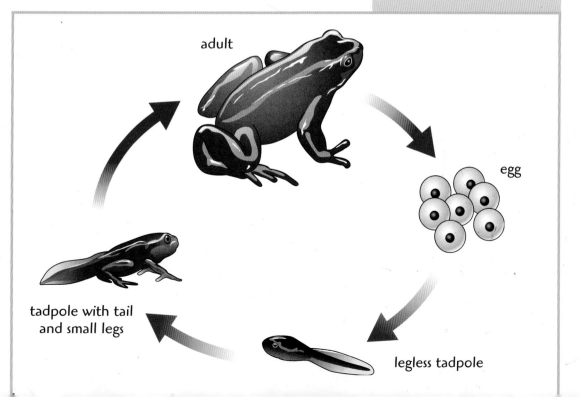

adult

egg

legless tadpole

tadpole with tail and small legs

Fact File

What is . . .

• the fastest and slowest *metamorphosis?*
Gray tree frogs take just one month to change from egg to young frog. Mountain yellow-legged frogs may take three to four years if they live in cold water.

• the oldest individual?
The oldest known toad, a common toad, lived 40 years, and the oldest known salamander, a Japanese giant salamander, lived to be 55 years old.

• the biggest individual?

Species	Body length	Weight
Chinese giant salamander	6 ft (1.8 m)	143 lb (65 kg)
Caecilian	5 ft (1.5 m)	unknown
Goliath frog	12 in. (30 cm)	$7\frac{1}{4}$ lb (3.3 kg)

• the smallest individual?
The smallest adult amphibian is a Brazilian gold frog, which is less than a half inch (one centimeter) long.

What was the first amphibian?

By studying fossils, scientists have figured out that the first amphibians lived on Earth about 360 million years ago—earlier than dinosaurs. Amphibians were the first **vertebrates** to live on land.

Amphibian Classification

Different amphibians can look as different as a tree frog and an axolotl. They are grouped together because they are similar in some ways, such as their skin that has no scales or hair, their skeletons, and the way they **breed** and change as they grow. There are three amphibian families:

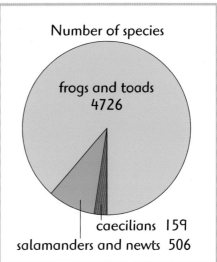

Number of species

frogs and toads
4726

caecilians 159

salamanders and newts 506

- Frogs and toads. All have large heads and short bodies. Toads are very much like frogs, but their skin is rougher and their back legs are shorter.
- Salamanders and newts. Newts are just one type of salamander. Other types of salamanders range from tiny ones with gripping tails that live in trees to giant salamanders that grow up to 5 feet (1.5 meters) long.
- Caecilians. Although they look more like big earthworms than frogs, caecilians are **burrowing** animals that have a lot of similarities to other amphibians.

Within each family, there are smaller groups whose members are similar in some way. For example, several hundred known **species** of frogs are grouped together as tree frogs because they all have sticky fingers shaped for climbing trees.

Glossary

adapted word to describe a plant or animal, or a part of one, that has gradually changed over time to make it better able to live in its habitat

blood vessels tubes in the body through which blood flows

breed have babies

bromeliad plant that grows on another plant for support and collects rainwater in waxy, cup-shaped leaves

burrow home of an underground animal; process of digging underground

camouflage colors or patterns that help an animal blend in with its background

captivity being kept in a zoo or cage, unable to get out

carnivores meat-eating animals

cocoon protective covering

courtship special behavior that prepares animals for mating

digest break down food in the body so that it can be used for energy

embryo unborn or unhatched young

environment animal's surroundings, including plants and other animals that live there

extinct vanished completely

fertilize cause an egg and sperm to join, which leads to the development of an embryo

gills body parts used for breathing underwater

habitat place where a plant or animal lives

herbivores animals that eat plants

hibernate sleep deeply through the winter

inherit to be born with features that are or become the same as those of the parents

irrigate water land to grow crops

larvae young animals that look very different from their parents, for example, tadpoles

mammal warm-blooded animal with a backbone that feeds its young on milk from the mother's body

metamorphosis change of shape during an animal's life cycle

migration regular movement of animals from one place to another, usually in search of food or a place to breed

mucus slimy, sticky liquid produced by amphibians

oxygen element in the air and in water that living things need to breathe

predator animal that hunts or catches other animals for food

prey animals that are hunted or caught for food by predators

shed lose skin that will be replaced

species type of living thing. Male and female animals of the same species can breed to produce healthy babies.

sperm type of cell made by male animals that joins with an egg in fertilization

survival staying alive

territory area within a habitat that an animal claims as its own

tropical rain forest thick forests of tall trees that grow in hot places where it rains daily

urinate to release a waste liquid called urine from the body

vertebrate animal with backbone

vocal sac skin near throat that can expand to help an amphibian make sounds

webbed word used to describe feet that have skin between the toes to help animals move through water

yolk part of an egg that serves as food for the baby growing inside

More Books to Read

Harvey, Bev. *Amphibians.* Broomall, Mass.: Chelsea House Publishers, 2003.

Heinrichs, Ann. *Frogs.* Minneapolis, Minn.: Compass Point Books, 2003.

Murray, Julie. *Salamanders.* Minneapolis, Minn.: ABDO Publishing Company, 2003.

Murray, Julie. *Toads.* Minneapolis, Minn.: ABDO Publishing Company, 2002.

Miller, Sara Swan. *Salamanders: Secret, Silent Lives.* Danbury, Conn.: Scholastic Library Publishing, 2000.

Zemlicka, Shannon. *From Tadpole to Frog.* Minneapolis, Minn.: Lerner Publishing Group, 2002.

Index

axolotl 11, 21

baby amphibians 5, 7–10
body temperature 17, 18
breathing 4, 8, 12, 14, 17
breeding 19–24, 27
breeding territory 21
bullfrogs 12, 13, 15
burrows 17, 18

caecilians 4, 7, 11, 14, 17, 24, 28
camouflage 16
carnivores 13
cold-blooded animals 4, 18
courtship calls 21, 22
courtship displays 21

dangers 9, 15–16, 25, 26
defenses 15–16

earliest amphibians 28
eggs 5–6, 7, 9, 10, 23, 24, 27
extinction 26

food and feeding 9, 13–14
frogs 4, 5, 6, 7, 8, 9, 10, 11, 12, 13, 14,
    15, 16, 18, 19, 21, 22, 23, 24, 28

gills 4, 8, 11, 12, 17

habitats 26
hibernation 18

inherited features 25

larvae 7, 8, 9, 10, 11, 13, 20, 27
life cycle 27
life span 25, 28

mating 20, 21, 22, 23, 27
metamorphosis 11, 12, 19, 27, 28
migration 20
mucus 4, 15

newts 4, 8, 13, 15, 16, 19, 20, 21,
    24, 28

poison 3, 16,
pollution 26
predators 9, 15, 22, 25

salamanders 4, 7, 11, 13, 14, 15, 16,
    19, 21, 23, 24, 25, 28
senses 14
size and weight 28
skin 4, 16, 17, 18, 24
species of amphibian 4, 28

tadpoles 8, 10, 11, 12, 13
tails 4, 11, 12, 21
toads 4, 6, 8, 11, 13, 14, 17, 20, 21,
    22, 23, 24, 27, 28

vertebrates 4

webbed feet 12, 15